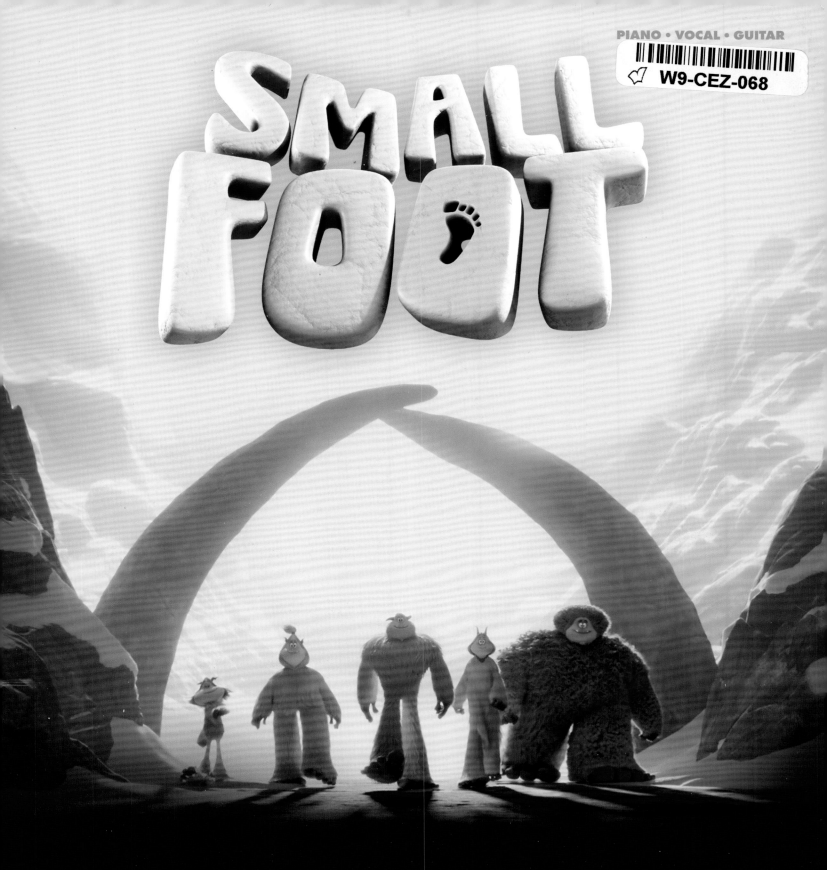

SMALL FOOT

Alfred

Produced by
Alfred Music
P.O. Box 10003
Van Nuys, CA 91410-0003
alfred.com

Printed in USA.

ISBN-10: 1-4706-4150-X
ISBN-13: 978-1-4706-4150-4

PERFECTION

Words and Music by
WAYNE KIRKPATRICK and KAREY KIRKPATRICK

Perfection - 6 - 1

8

not one lit-tle thing,_ I mean_be-cause I do what the stones_say and I'm do-ing o - kay.

What could be bet - ter than this?_ It is what it is._ It is_ per-fec - tion._

2. Look at ev-'ry-bod-y

Verse 2:

do their part, and they do it with a hap - py_heart, and it gives them all a sense_ of great-er

WONDERFUL QUESTIONS

Words and Music by
WAYNE KIRKPATRICK and KAREY KIRKPATRICK

Villagers: "What does it eat? How does it think with a little tiny brain?"   Migo: "Honestly, I have just as many questions as you do."

Villagers: "Where is its horn? Is that his ear? Does it want a bit of fruit?
How is it here? Because the stone says it can't be?"

Migo:

It's

Wonderful Questions - 5 - 1

24

26

LET IT LIE

Words and Music by
WAYNE KIRKPATRICK and
KAREY KIRKPATRICK

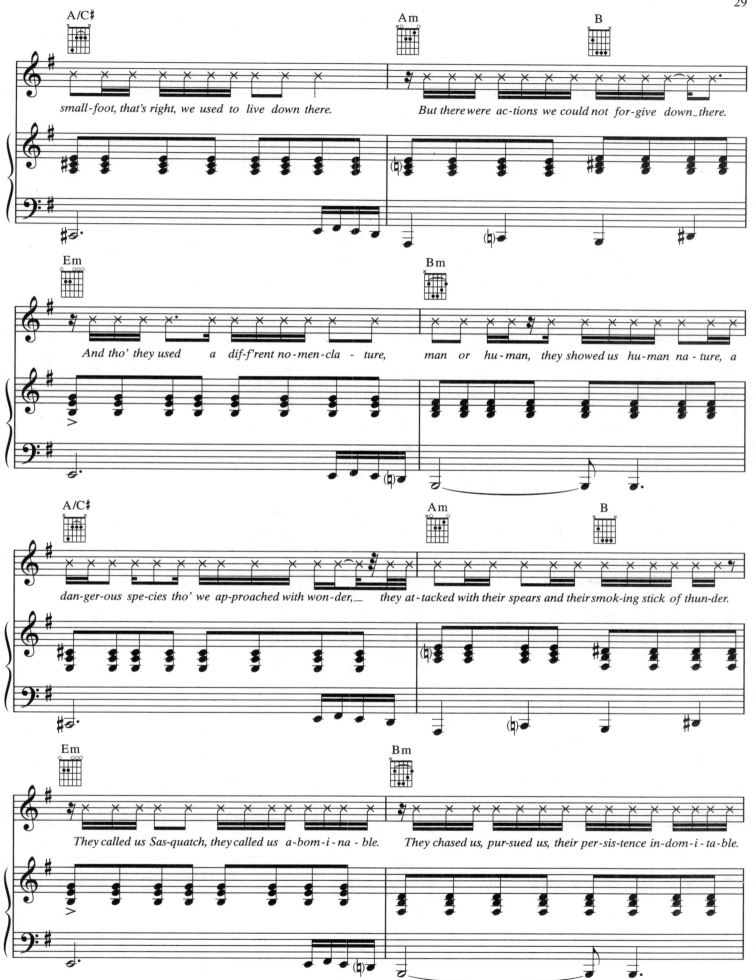

34

So let me share a se-cret that you'll learn as you grow old-er. What's true or not true is in the eye of the be-hold-er.

So do you want to pre-vent our own an-ni-hi-la-tion? Yes! Then our on-ly goal should be to con-trol the flow of in-for-ma-tion.

Un-less you want to see the small-foot con-quer and pil-lage. No! Then pro-tect the lie   and you pro-tect the

vil-lage.   Lives are at stake, Migo.   Your friends.   Your father.   Meechee.

37

Let It Lie - 10 - 10

MOMENT OF TRUTH

Words and Music by
WAYNE KIRKPATRICK and KAREY KIRKPATRICK

Rock, quasi "hand jive" ♩ = 105

Verse 1 (Sing 1st time only):

Verse 2 (Sing 2nd time only):

40

Chorus:

change, we got-ta come to-geth-er, me and you, in a mo oh oh oh

mo-ment of truth. If it's ev-er gon-na change, we got-ta come to-geth-er, me and you, in a

mo oh oh oh mo-ment of truth. Na na na na na na na na na na

na na na. Ye-i oh oh whoa oh whoa oh oh. Na na na na na

Moment of Truth - 6 - 3

42

Chorus:

FINALLY FREE

Words and Music
NIALL HORAN, JULIAN BUNETTA, JOHN RYAN,
ALEXANDER IZQUIERDO, IAN ZACHARY FRANZINO,
ANDREW HASS and TOBIA JESSO JR.

Finally Free - 8 - 1

Verse 2:

48

Finally Free - 8 - 5

50